PERM

Electronic Labor Certifications for Employment Petitions

Attorney Brian D. Lerner

BDL LAW OFFICES OF BRIAN D. LERNER A PROFESSIONAL CORPORATION

ATTORNEY DRAFTED IMMIGRATION PETITIONS

By

Brian D. Lerner

Attorney at Law

Disclaimer and Terms of Use:

Effort has been made to ensure that the information in this book is accurate and complete. However, the author and the publisher do not warrant that this particular petition will mirror or be exactly as your situation. There has not been any attorney-client agreement created by the purchase of this petition or application. No legal advice has occurred. The cases, regulations and/or statutes cited may change at any time without notice.

ISBN: 978-1-958990-03-2

INTRODUCTION

There are a multitude of different immigration petitions and applications. They are complex and full of requirements. Obviously, it would be best to hire an immigration attorney to best prepare the petitions and applications. However, this can certainly cost thousands of dollars.

The next best option is to get a sample of the petition written by an experienced immigration attorney. The samples cost a fraction what would be charged by an immigration attorney. However, while the reader has to alter, amend and change the parts of the sample petition to reflect their actual situation, it is a fantastic roadmap for them to use. If the reader has purchased the entire petition or application, they will have real live samples of cover letters, forms, declarations, affidavits and the necessary exhibits to use. The samples come from real cases and the names of those clients have been redacted to protect the privacy of that person or corporation.

These are petitions and applications that have been drafted by an experienced immigration attorney with over 25 years of experience. Get the benefits of that experience without the costs.

CONTENTS

About the Law Offices of Brian D. Lerner

Brian D. Lerner has been a licensed attorney since 1992 and started the Law Offices of Brian D. Lerner, APC. The law practice consists of Immigration and Nationality Law and everything involved with and regarding immigration which includes citizenship, investment visas, family and employment visas, removal and deportation hearings, appeals, waivers, adjustment, consulate processing and all types of immigration and citizenship matters. Thousands of families have been reunited and/or permitted to stay in the U.S. and/or return to the U.S. because of the successful work of Immigration Attorney Brian D. Lerner.

This law offices handles all types of immigration cases including family based and employment based. Immigration issues range from immigration court proceedings to trying to fix what paralegals may have done that was neither correct nor proper. Foreign nationals must have experience lawyers admitted to practice law.

The Law Offices of Brian D. Lerner, APC, handles cases arising from business visas, work permits, Green Cards, non-immigrant visas, deportation, citizenship, appeals and all areas of immigration. The Law Offices of Brian D. Lerner, APC does EB-5 Investor Visas, H-1B Specialty Occupation, L-1 Intracompany Transferee, E-2 Treaty Investor, E-1 Treaty Trader, O-1 Extraordinary Ability among others. Regarding immigrant visas for the Green Card, the firm does PERM and advanced degree PERM, Family Petitions, and Extraordinary Alien Petitions. In addition to affirmative petitions, the Law Firm represents people in people in deportation and removal hearings, including political asylum, withholding of removal, and convention against torture cases.

Brian D. Lerner has been certified as an expert in Immigration & Nationality Law by the California State Bar, Board of Legal Specialization since 2000 and has been re-certified three times. He now passes on his decades of experience by allowing the Reader, Law Schools, Professors and other Immigration Attorneys to purchase sample petitions on every facet of Immigration Law.

About the Program Electronic Review Management (PERM)

PERM is the system used for obtaining Labor Certification and is the first step for certain Foreign Nationals in obtaining an employment-based immigrant visa. The PERM is an application filed with the Department of Labor to establish that there are no willing and qualified United States workers in the United States. It is the first part of the employment based immigration process.

Program Electronic Review Management (PERM)

ETA Form 9089

OMB Approval: 1205-0451
Expiration Date: 11/30/2017

Application for Permanent Employment Certification

ETA Form 9089

U.S. Department of Labor

Please read and review the filing instructions before completing this form. A copy of the instructions can be found at http://www.foreignlaborcert.doleta.gov/pdf/9089inst.pdf

Employing or continuing to employ an alien unauthorized to work in the United States is illegal and may subject the employer to criminal prosecution, civil money penalties, or both.

A. Refiling Instructions

1. Are you seeking to utilize the filing date from a previously submitted Application for Alien Employment Certification (ETA 750)?	☐ Yes ☑ No
1-A. If Yes, enter the previous filing date	
1-B. Indicate the previous SWA or local office case number OR if not available, specify state where case was originally filed:	

B. Schedule A or Sheepherder Information

1. Is this application in support of a Schedule A or Sheepherder Occupation?	☐ Yes ☑ No
If Yes, do NOT send this application to the Department of Labor. All applications in support of Schedule A or Sheepherder Occupations must be sent directly to the appropriate Department of Homeland Security office.	

C. Employer Information (Headquarters or Main Office)

1. Employer's name CONSULTANTS [redacted]			
2. Address 1 [redacted]. SPECTRUM CENTER BLVD.			
Address 2 [redacted]			
3. City SAN DIEGO	State/Province CA 1985	Country UNITED STATES OF AMERICA	Postal code 92123
4. Phone number [redacted]		Extension	
5. Number of employees 1		6. Year commenced business 2016	
7. FEIN(Federal Employer Identification Number) [redacted]		8. NAICS Code 611710	
9. Is the employer a closely held corporation, partnership, or sole proprietorship in which the alien has an ownership interest, or is there a familial relationship between the owners, stockholders, partners, corporate officers, or incorporators, and the alien?			☐ Yes ☑ No

D. Employer Contact Information (This section must be filled out. This information must be different from the agent or attorney information listed in Section E).

1. Contact's last name [redacted]	First name [redacted]	Middle initial [redacted]	
2. Address 1 [redacted]			
Address 2 [redacted]			
3. City San Diego	State/Province CA	Country UNITED STATES OF AMERICA	Postal code
4. Phone number [redacted]		Extension	
5. E-mail address [redacted]			

E. Agent or Attorney Information (If applicable)

1. Agent or attorney's last name Lerner	First name Brian		Middle initial D
2. Firm name Law Offices of Brian D. Lerner, APC			
3. Firm EIN 331012936	4. Phone number 5624950554	Extension	
5. Address 1 3233 E. Broadway			
Address 2			
6. City Long Beach	State/Province CA	Country UNITED STATES OF AMERICA	Postal code 90803
7. E-mail address blerner@californiaimmigration.us			

F. Prevailing Wage Information (as provided by the State Workforce Agency)

1. Prevailing wage tracking number (if applicable)	2. SOC/O*NET(OES) code
3. Occupation Title	4. Skill Level Level II
5. Prevailing wage $	Per: (Choose only one) ☐ Hour ☐ Week ☐ Bi-Weekly ☐ Month ☑ Year
6. Prevailing wage source (Choose only one) ☑ OES ☐ CBA ☐ Employer Conducted Survey ☐ DBA ☐ SCA ☐ Other	
6-A. If Other is indicated in question 6, specify:	
7. Determination date 04/25/2017	8. Expiration date 07/24/2017

G. Wage Offer Information

1. Offered wage From: $	To: (Optional)	Per: (Choose only one) ☐ Hour ☐ Week ☐ Bi-Weekly ☐ Month ☑ Year

H. Job Opportunity Information (Where work will be performed)

1. Primary worksite (where work is to be performed) address 1		
Address 2 █████████		
2. City San Diego	State CA	Postal code
3. Job title		
4. Education: minimum level required: ☐ None ☐ High School ☐ Associate's ☑ Bachelor's ☐ Master's ☐ Doctorate ☐ Other		
4-A. If Other is indicated in question 4, specify the education required:		
4-B. Major field of study Public Relations, Communications, Etc.		
5. Is training required for the job opportunity? ☐ Yes ☑ No	5-A. If Yes, number of months of training required:	

H. Job Opportunity Information Continued

5-B. Indicate the field of training:

6. Is experience in the job offered required for the job? ☑ Yes ☐ No

6-A. If Yes, number of months experience required: 3

7. Is there an alternate field of study that is acceptable? ☐ Yes ☑ No

7-A. If Yes, specify the major field of study:

8. Is there an alternate combination of education and experience that is acceptable? ☑ Yes ☐ No

8-A. If Yes, specify the alternate level of education required:
☐ None ☐ High School ☐ Associate's ☐ Bachelor's ☐ Master's ☐ Doctorate ☑ Other

8-B. If Other is indicated in question 8-A, indicate the alternate level of education required:
High School plus 2 Years Related Experience

8-C. If applicable, indicate the number of years experience acceptable in question 8:
2

9. Is a foreign educational equivalent acceptable? ☑ Yes ☐ No

10. Is experience in an alternate occupation acceptable? ☐ Yes ☑ No

10-A. If Yes, number of months experience in alternate occupation required:

10-B. Identify the job title of the acceptable alternate occupation:

11. Job duties – If submitting by mail, add attachment if necessary. Job duties description must begin in this space.
See Attachment

12. Are the job opportunity's requirements normal for the occupation? ☑ Yes ☐ No

If the answer to this question is No, the employer must be prepared to provide documentation demonstrating that the job requirements are supported by business necessity.

13. Is knowledge of a foreign language required to perform the job duties? ☐ Yes ☑ No

If the answer to this question is Yes, the employer must be prepared to provide documentation demonstrating that the language requirements are supported by business necessity.

14. Specific skills or other requirements – If submitting by mail, add attachment if necessary. Skills description must begin in this space.
See Attachment

H. Job Opportunity Information Continued

15. Does this application involve a job opportunity that includes a combination of occupations?	☐ Yes ☑ No
16. Is the position identified in this application being offered to the alien identified in Section J?	☑ Yes ☐ No
17. Does the job require the alien to live on the employer's premises?	☐ Yes ☑ No
18. Is the application for a live-in household domestic service worker?	☐ Yes ☑ No
18-A. If Yes, have the employer and the alien executed the required employment contract and has the employer provided a copy of the contract to the alien?	☐ Yes ☐ No ☐ NA

I. Recruitment Information

a. Occupation Type – All must complete this section.

1. Is this application for a **professional occupation**, other than a college or university teacher? Professional occupations are those for which a bachelor's degree (or equivalent) is normally required.	☑ Yes ☐ No
2. Is this application for a college or university teacher? **If Yes, complete questions 2-A and 2-B below.**	☐ Yes ☑ No
2-A. Did you select the candidate using a competitive recruitment and selection process?	☐ Yes ☐ No
2-B. Did you use the basic recruitment process for professional occupations?	☐ Yes ☐ No

b. Special Recruitment and Documentation Procedures for College and University Teachers – Complete only if the answer to question I.a.2-A is Yes.

3. Date alien selected:
4. Name and date of national professional journal in which advertisement was placed:
5. Specify additional recruitment information in this space. Add an attachment if necessary.

c. Professional/Non-Professional Information – Complete this section unless your answer to question B.1 or I.a.2-A is YES.

6. Start date for the SWA job order	7. End date for the SWA job order 09/06/2017
8. Is there a Sunday edition of the newspaper in the area of intended employment?	☑ Yes ☐ No
9. Name of newspaper (of general circulation) in which the first advertisement was placed:	
10. Date of first advertisement identified in question 9: 07/09/2017	
11. Name of newspaper or professional journal (if applicable) in which second advertisement was placed: San Diego Union Tribune	☑ Newspaper ☐ Journal

I. Recruitment Information Continued

12. Date of second newspaper advertisement or date of publication of journal identified in question 11: 07/16/2017

d. Professional Recruitment Information – Complete if the answer to question I.a.1 is YES or if the answer to I.a.2-B is YES. Complete at least 3 of the items.

13. Dates advertised at job fair From: To:	14. Dates of on-campus recruiting From: To:
15. Dates posted on employer web site From: 07/18/2017 To: 09/11/2017	16. Dates advertised with trade or professional organization From: To:
17. Dates listed with job search web site From: 07/19/2017 To: 07/20/2017	18. Dates listed with private employment firm From: To:
19. Dates advertised with employee referral program From: To:	20. Dates advertised with campus placement office From: To:
21. Dates advertised with local or ethnic newspaper From: 07/27/2017 To: 08/02/2017	22. Dates advertised with radio or TV ads From: To:

e. General Information – All must complete this section.

23. Has the employer received payment of any kind for the submission of this application?	☐ Yes ☑ No
23-A. If Yes, describe details of the payment including the amount, date and purpose of the payment :	
24. Has the bargaining representative for workers in the occupation in which the alien will be employed been provided with notice of this filing at least 30 days but not more than 180 days before the date the application is filed?	☐ Yes ☐ No ☑ NA
25. If there is no bargaining representative, has a notice of this filing been posted for 10 business days in a conspicuous location at the place of employment, ending at least 30 days before but not more than 180 days before the date the application is filed?	☑ Yes ☐ No ☐ NA
26. Has the employer had a layoff in the area of intended employment in the occupation involved in this application or in a related occupation within the six months immediately preceding the filing of this application?	☐ Yes ☑ No
26-A. If Yes, were the laid off U.S. workers notified and considered for the job opportunity for which certification is sought?	☐ Yes ☐ No ☐ NA

J. Alien Information (This section must be filled out. This information must be different from the agent or attorney information listed in Section E).

1. Alien's last name [redacted]	First name [redacted]	Full middle name	
2. Current address 1 [redacted]			
Address 2			
3. City [redacted]	State/Province [redacted]	Country	Postal code 68101
4. Phone number of current residence [redacted]			
5. Country of citizenship	6. Country of birth [redacted]		
7. Alien's date of birth	8. Class of admission Not in USA		
9. Alien registration number (A#)	10. Alien admission number (I-94)		
11. Education: highest level achieved as required by the requested job opportunity: ☐ None ☑ High School ☐ Associate's ☐ Bachelor's ☐ Master's ☐ Doctorate ☐ Other			

J. Alien Information Continued

11-A. If Other indicated in question 11, specify	
12. Specify major field(s) of study	
13. Year relevant education completed 2001	
14. Institution where relevant education specified in question 11 was received	
15. Address 1 of conferring institution	
Address 2	
16. City / State/Province / Country / Postal code	
17. Did the alien complete the training required for the requested job opportunity, as indicated in question H.5?	☐ Yes ☐ No ☑ NA
18. Does the alien have the experience as required for the requested job opportunity indicated in question H.6?	☑ Yes ☐ No ☐ NA
19. Does the alien possess the alternate combination of education and experience as indicated in question H.8?	☑ Yes ☐ No ☐ NA
20. Does the alien have the experience in an alternate occupation specified in question H.10?	☐ Yes ☐ No ☑ NA
21. Did the alien gain any of the qualifying experience with the employer in a position substantially comparable to the job opportunity requested?	☐ Yes ☑ No ☐ NA
22. Did the employer pay for any of the alien's education or training necessary to satisfy any of the employer's job requirements for this position?	☐ Yes ☑ No
23. Is the alien currently employed by the petitioning employer?	☑ Yes ☐ No

K. Alien Work Experience

List all jobs the alien has held during the past 3 years. Also list any other experience that qualifies the alien for the job opportunity for which the employer is seeking certification.

a. Job 1

1. Employer name			
2. Address 1 [redacted]			
Address 2			
3. City Los Angeles	State/Province CA	Country UNITED STATES OF AMERICA	Postal code
4. Type of business Consulate		5. Job title Consular Assistant	
6. Start date 05/01/2012	7. End date 04/28/2017	8. Number of hours worked per week 35	

Job 1 continued on next page

K. Alien Work Experience Continued

9. Job details (duties performed, use of tools, machines, equipment, skills, qualifications, certifications, licenses, etc. Include the phone number of the employer and the name of the alien's supervisor.)

See Attachment

b. Job 2

1. Employer name	
2. Address 1	
Address 2	
3. City	Tel Aviv-Yafo
State/Province	
Country	
Postal code	
4. Type of business	Hoteliery and Hospitality
5. Job title	Guest Relations Representa
6. Start date	12/01/2004
7. End date	04/30/2006
8. Number of hours worked per week	45

9. Job details (duties performed, use of tools, machines, equipment, skills, qualifications, certifications, licenses, etc. Include the phone number of the employer and the name of the alien's supervisor.)

See Attachment

c. Job 3

1. Employer name	
2. Address 1	
Address 2	
3. City	Tel Aviv
State/Province	
Country	
Postal code	6380501
4. Type of business	
5. Job title	Marketing Representative
6. Start date	02/01/2004
7. End date	01/30/2005
8. Number of hours worked per week	45

Job 3 continued on next page

K. Alien Work Experience Continued

9. Job details (duties performed, use of tools, machines, equipment, skills, qualifications, certifications, licenses, etc. Include the phone number of the employer and the name of the alien's supervisor.)

See Attachment

L. Alien Declaration

I declare under penalty of perjury that Sections J and K are true and correct. *I understand that to knowingly furnish false information in the preparation of this form and any supplement thereto or to aid, abet, or counsel another to do so is a federal offense punishable by a fine or imprisonment up to five years or both under 18 U.S.C. §§ 2 and 1001. Other penalties apply as well to fraud or misuse of ETA immigration documents and to perjury with respect to such documents under 18 U.S.C. §§ 1546 and 1621.*

In addition, I ***further declare*** *under penalty of perjury that I intend to accept the position offered in Section H of this application if a labor certification is approved and I am granted a visa or an adjustment of status based on this application.*

1. Alien's last name	First name	Full middle name
ISRAELI	MARCELLE	
2. Signature	Date signed	

Note – The signature and date signed do not have to be filled out when electronically submitting to the Department of Labor for processing, but must be complete when submitting by mail. If the application is submitted electronically, any resulting certification MUST be signed *immediately upon receipt* from DOL before it can be submitted to USCIS for final processing.

M. Declaration of Preparer

1. **Was the application completed by the employer?** If No, you must complete this section	☐ Yes	☑ No

I hereby certify that I have prepared this application at the direct request of the employer listed in Section C and that to the best of my knowledge the information contained herein is true and correct. *I understand that to knowingly furnish false information in the preparation of this form and any supplement thereto or to aid, abet, or counsel another to do so is a federal offense punishable by a fine, imprisonment up to five years or both under 18 U.S.C. §§ 2 and 1001. Other penalties apply as well to fraud or misuse of ETA immigration documents and to perjury with respect to such documents under 18 U.S.C. §§ 1546 and 1621.*

2. Preparer's last name	First name	Middle initial
Lerner	Brian	D
3. Title: Attorney		
4. E-mail address: blerner@californiaimmigration.us		
5. Signature	Date signed	

Note – The signature and date signed do not have to be filled out when electronically submitting to the Department of Labor for processing, but must be complete when submitting by mail. If the application is submitted electronically, any resulting certification MUST be signed *immediately upon receipt* from DOL before it can be submitted to USCIS for final processing.

N. Employer Declaration

By virtue of my signature below, ***I HEREBY CERTIFY*** *the following conditions of employment:*

1. The offered wage equals or exceeds the prevailing wage and I will pay at least the prevailing wage.
2. The wage is not based on commissions, bonuses or other incentives, unless I guarantees a wage paid on a weekly, bi-weekly, or monthly basis that equals or exceeds the prevailing wage.
3. I have enough funds available to pay the wage or salary offered the alien.
4. I will be able to place the alien on the payroll on or before the date of the alien's proposed entrance into the United States.
5. The job opportunity does not involve unlawful discrimination by race, creed, color, national origin, age, sex, religion, handicap, or citizenship.
6. The job opportunity is not:
   a. Vacant because the former occupant is on strike or is being locked out in the course of a labor dispute involving a work stoppage; or
   b. At issue in a labor dispute involving a work stoppage.
7. The job opportunity's terms, conditions, and occupational environment are not contrary to Federal, state or local law.
8. The job opportunity has been and is clearly open to any U.S. worker.
9. The U.S. workers who applied for the job opportunity were rejected for lawful job-related reasons.
10. The job opportunity is for full-time, permanent employment for an employer other than the alien.

I hereby designate the agent or attorney identified in section E (if any) to represent me for the purpose of labor certification and, by virtue of my signature in Block 3 below, **I take full responsibility** for the accuracy of any representations made by my agent or attorney.

I declare under penalty of perjury that I have read and reviewed this application and that to the best of my knowledge the information contained herein is true and accurate. *I understand that to knowingly furnish false information in the preparation of this form and any supplement thereto or to aid, abet, or counsel another to do so is a federal offense punishable by a fine or imprisonment up to five years or both under 18 U.S.C. §§ 2 and 1001. Other penalties apply as well to fraud or misuse of ETA immigration documents and to perjury with respect to such documents under 18 U.S.C. §§ 1546 and 1621.*

1. Last name	First name	Middle initial
[redacted]	[redacted]	S
2. Title President and Founder		
3. Signature	Date signed	

Note – The signature and date signed do not have to be filled out when electronically submitting to the Department of Labor for processing, but must be complete when submitting by mail. If the application is submitted electronically, any resulting certification MUST be signed *immediately upon receipt* from DOL before it can be submitted to USCIS for final processing.

O. U.S. Government Agency Use Only

Pursuant to the provisions of Section 212 (a)(5)(A) of the Immigration and Nationality Act, as amended, I hereby certify that there are not sufficient U.S. workers available and the employment of the above will not adversely affect the wages and working conditions of workers in the U.S. similarly employed.

This Certification is valid from ____________ to ____________

Signature of Certifying Officer   Date   Signed

[redacted]   10/23/2017

Case Number   Filing Date

P. OMB Information *Paperwork Reduction Act Information Control Number 1205-0451*

Persons are not required to respond to this collection of information unless it displays a currently valid OMB control number.

Respondent's reply to these reporting requirements is required to obtain the benefits of permanent employment certification (Immigration and Nationality Act, Section 212(a)(5)). Public reporting burden for this collection of information is estimated to average 1¼ hours per response, including the time for reviewing instructions, searching existing data sources, gathering and maintaining the data needed, and completing and reviewing the collection of information. Send comments regarding this burden estimate to the Division of Foreign Labor Certification * U.S. Department of Labor * Room C4312 * 200 Constitution Ave., NW * Washington, DC * 20210.

Do NOT send the completed application to this address.

Q. Privacy Statement Information

In accordance with the Privacy Act of 1974, as amended (5 U.S.C. 552a), you are hereby notified that the information provided herein is protected under the Privacy Act. The Department of Labor (Department or DOL) maintains a System of Records titled Employer Application and Attestation File for Permanent and Temporary Alien Workers (DOL/ETA-7) that includes this record.

Under routine uses for this system of records, case files developed in processing labor certification applications, labor condition applications, or labor attestations may be released as follows: in connection with appeals of denials before the DOL Office of Administrative Law Judges and Federal courts, records may be released to the employers that filed such applications, their representatives, to named alien beneficiaries or their representatives, and to the DOL Office of Administrative Law Judges and Federal courts; and in connection with administering and enforcing immigration laws and regulations, records may be released to such agencies as the DOL Office of Inspector General, Employment Standards Administration, the Department of Homeland Security, and the Department of State.

Further relevant disclosures may be made in accordance with the Privacy Act and under the following circumstances: in connection with federal litigation; for law enforcement purposes; to authorized parent locator persons under Pub. L. 93-647; to an information source or public authority in connection with personnel, security clearance, procurement, or benefit-related matters; to a contractor or their employees, grantees or their employees, consultants, or volunteers who have been engaged to assist the agency in the performance of Federal activities; for Federal debt collection purposes; to the Office of Management and Budget in connection with its legislative review, coordination, and clearance activities; to a Member of Congress or their staff in response to an inquiry of the Congressional office made at the written request of the subject of the record; in connection with records management; and to the news media and the public when a matter under investigation becomes public knowledge, the Solicitor of Labor determines the disclosure is necessary to preserve confidence in the integrity of the Department, or the Solicitor of Labor determines that a legitimate public interest exists in the disclosure of information, unless the Solicitor of Labor determines that disclosure would constitute an unwarranted invasion of personal privacy.

Addendum

H. 11. Job duties

Responding to requests for information about company and its products and services; Preparing advertising, marketing and information materials to promote a company and its products and services; Establishing or maintaining cooperative relationships with representatives of community, consumer, employee, or public interest groups; Planning or directing, development or communication of programs to maintain favorable public perceptions of a company and its products and services; Studying the objectives and needs of a company to develop public relations strategies that will influence public opinion or promote ideas, products, or services; Updating and maintaining marketing, advertising and promotional materials; Conferring with management to identify trends, interests or concerns or identify potential clients; Arranging public appearances, lectures, contests, parties or exhibits to increase product or service awareness or to promote goodwill; Preparing or delivering presentations/speeches to further public relations objectives; Conferring with support personnel to produce or coordinate production of advertisements marketing or promotional material; and Consulting with advertising agencies or staff to arrange promotional campaigns.

Addendum

H.14. Specific skills or other requirements

Responding to requests for information about company/employer and its products and services; Preparing advertising, marketing and information materials to promote a company/employer and its products and services; Establishing or maintaining cooperative relationships with representatives of community, consumer, employee, or public interest groups; Planning or directing development or communication of programs to maintain favorable public perceptions of a company/employer and its
products and services; Studying the objectives and needs of a company/employer to develop public relations strategies that will influence public opinion or promote ideas, products, or services;
Updating and maintaining marketing, advertising and promotional materials; Conferring with management to identify trends, interests or concerns or identify potential clients; Arranging public appearances, lectures, contests, parties or exhibits to increase product or service awareness or to
promote goodwill; Preparing or delivering presentations/speeches to further public relations objectives; Conferring with support personnel to produce or coordinate production of advertisements marketing or promotional material; and Consulting with advertising agencies or staff
to arrange promotional campaigns.

Addendum

K. 9. Job 1 - Job Details

Providing information about the consulte's services; Training both existing and new employees; Dealing with high volume of clients with different needs and directing or providing them with the relevant service providers/ organizations; Preparing, examining and approving variety of visa; Obtaining legal documentations from Israeli officials; Delivering presentations in Consular Department meetings; Preparing and examining passport applications and directing citizens to participate in relevant programs if qualified; Creating personalized profile, accompanying and supporting Israeli citizens throughout their applications, maintaining professional costumer-provider relationships; Testing new services in order to improve efficiency in the consular department; Assisting in planing and executing initiatives to reach the target audience through appropriate channels in order to engage them with relevant activities/special programs/ events offered for visitors/ citizens; Assisting in collaborating with professionals and Jewish organizations to coordinate awareness among the relevant community; Participating in collaboration with vendors to execute promotional Israeli/Jewish events and presenting advertising materials; promoting ideas and services,both individually and in community events, to support relationships with leaders/agencies in the Jewish community in Los Angeles .

Addendum

K. 9. Job 2 - Job Details

Ensuring VIP guests are satisfied with their stay; Coordinating between the different departments to meet vip guests' specific needs; Selling and distribution of membership card and loyalty program (priority club) to variety of clients attending the hotel; Maintaining and presenting promotional materials of the hotel offered services; Analyzing customer feedback and providing strategic direction to continuously improve overall rating, and delivering those presentations in meetings; Training new employees at the department; Identify potential guest in the hotel and offer/market exclusive and extended VIP services, as well as membership program; Creating and maintaining professional costumer-provider relationships with individuals or companies that use the hotel VIP and guest relations services; Maintaining professional relations with VIP clients during their stay and also thereafter throughout the year to ensure returning costumers; Ensuring special guests receive personalized services and establish relations with them; Promoting all hotel amenities, conveniences and programs offered; Directing and communicating programs to maintain perception of the hotel chain global services as well as distribution of the priority club membership and other local services.

Addendum

K. 9. Job 3 - Job Details

Presenting and arranging advertising materials for conferences, exhibitions and special events; Promoting services through media and commercial channels for clients; Coordinating all public relations activities and consulting with agents to produce campaigns; Organizing PR events to increase awareness of a company; Organizing and executing campaigns, as well as maintaining and updating promotional materials; Producing marketing materials, accessories, postal distribution, etc.; Conducting marketing tactics according to event type; Delivering reports and presentations on PR results.

Application for Prevailing Wage Determination

Form ETA - 9141

OMB Approval: 1205-0508
Expiration Date: 05/31/2019

Application for Prevailing Wage Determination
Form ETA-9141
U.S. Department of Labor

Please read and review the instructions carefully before completing this form and print legibly. A copy of the instructions can be found at http://www.foreignlaborcert.doleta.gov/.

A. Employment-Based Visa Information

1. Indicate the type of visa classification supported by this application *(Write classification symbol)*: *	PERM

B. Requestor Point-of-Contact Information

1. Contact's last (family) name *	2. First (given) name *	3. Middle name(s) *
LERNER	BRIAN	DAVID
4. Contact's job title * ATTORNEY		
5. Address 1 * 3233 E. BROADWAY		
6. Address 2 N/A		
7. City * LONG BEACH	8. State * CA	9. Postal code * 90803
10. Country * UNITED STATES OF AMERICA	11. Province (if applicable) N/A	
12. Telephone number * 562-495-0554	13. Extension N/A	14. Fax Number 562-608-8672
15. E-Mail Address BLERNER@CALIFORNIAIMMIGRATION.US		

C. Employer Information

1. Legal business name * Consultants for America's Veterans, LLC		
2. Trade name/Doing Business As (DBA), if applicable § N/A		
3. Address 1 * [redacted]		
4. Address 2 [redacted]		
5. City * [redacted]	6. State * CA	7. Postal code * 92123
8. Country * UNITED STATES OF AMERICA	9. Province (if applicable) N/A	
10. Telephone number * [redacted]	11. Extension N/A	
12. Federal Employer Identification Number (FEIN from IRS) * [redacted]	13. NAICS code (must be at least 4-digits) * 611710	

D. Wage Processing Information

1. Is the employer covered by ACWIA? * ❑ Yes ❑ No	
2. Is the position covered by a Collective Bargaining Agreement (CBA)? *	❑ Yes ❑ No
3. Is the employer requesting consideration of Davis-Bacon (DBA) or McNamara Service Contract (SCA) Acts? *	❑ Yes ❑ No ❑ DBA ❑ SCA

Form ETA-9141 **FOR DEPARTMENT OF LABOR USE ONLY** Page 1 of 5

Case Number: P-100-16325-078295 Case Status: IN PROCESS Validity Period: N/A to N/A

Application for Prevailing Wage Determination
Form ETA-9141
U.S. Department of Labor

D. Wage Processing Information (cont.)

4. Is the employer requesting consideration of a survey in determining the prevailing wage? *	☐ Yes ☐ No
4a. Survey Name: §	
4b. Survey date of publication: §	

E. Job Offer Information

a. Job Description:

1. Job Title * [redacted]	
2. *Suggested* SOC (ONET/OES) code * 27-3031	2a. *Suggested* SOC (ONET/OES) occupation title * Public Relations Specialists
3. Job Title of Supervisor for this Position (if applicable) § N/A	
4. Does this position supervise the work of other employees? * ☐ Yes ☒ No	4a. If "Yes", number of employees worker will supervise: § N/A
4b. If "Yes", please indicate the level of the employees to be supervised:	☐ Subordinate ☐ Peer

5. Job duties – Please provide a description of the duties to be performed with as much specificity as possible, including details regarding the areas/fields and/or products/industries involved. A description of the job duties to be performed **MUST** begin in this space. *

Job duties include:

- please see attached addendum.

6. Will travel be required in order to perform the job duties? * ☒ Yes ☐ No	6a. If "Yes", please provide details of the travel required, such as the area(s), frequency and nature of the travel. § SEE ADDENDUM

Case Number: P-100-16326-878299 Case Status: IN PROCESS Validity Period: N/A to N/A

OMB Approval: 1205-0466
Expiration Date: 05/31/2019

Application for Prevailing Wage Determination
Form ETA-9141
U.S. Department of Labor

E. Job Offer Information (cont.)

b. Minimum Job Requirements:

1. Education: minimum U.S. diploma/degree required *

☐ None ☐ High School/GED ☐ Associate's ☑ Bachelor's ☐ Master's ☐ Doctorate (PhD) ☐ Other degree (JD, MD, etc.)

1a. If "Other degree" in question 1, specify the diploma/degree required §	1b. Indicate the major(s) and/or field(s) of study required § (May list more than one related major and more than one field)
Or 2 Years Related Experience	Public Relations, Communications, Etc

2. Does the employer require a second U.S. diploma/degree? * ☐ Yes ☑ No

2a. If "Yes" in question 2, indicate the second U.S. diploma/degree and the major(s) and/or field(s) of study required §

N/A

3. Is training for the job opportunity required? * ☐ Yes ☑ No

3a. If "Yes" in question 3, specify the number of months of training required §	3b. Indicate the field(s)/name(s) of training required § (May list more than one related field and more than one type)
N/A	N/A

4. Is employment experience required? * ☑ Yes ☐ No

4a. If "Yes" in question 4, specify the number of months of experience required §	4b. Indicate the occupation required §
3	Public Relations Specialist

5. Special Requirements - List specific skills, licenses/certificates/certifications, and requirements of the job opportunity. *

Specific skills required: - please see attached addendum.

c. Place of Employment Information:

1. Worksite address 1 * [redacted]	
2. Address 2 [redacted]	
3. City * San Diego	4. County * SAN DIEGO
5. State/District/Territory * CA	6. Postal code * 92123
7. Will work be performed in multiple worksites within an area of intended employment or a location(s) other than the address listed above? *	☐ Yes ☐ No

7a. If "Yes", identify the geographic place(s) of employment indicating each metropolitan statistical area (MSA) or the independent city(ies)/township(s)/county(ies) (borough(s)/parish(es)) and the corresponding state(s) where work will be performed. If necessary, submit a second completed ETA Form 9141 with a listing of the additional anticipated worksites. Please note that wages cannot be provided for unspecified/unanticipated locations. §

N/A

Case Number: P-100-16326-078299 Case Status: IN PROCESS Validity Period: N/A to N/A

OMB Approval: 1205-0466
Expiration Date: 05/31/2019

Application for Prevailing Wage Determination
Form ETA-9141
U.S. Department of Labor

F. Prevailing Wage Determination

FOR OFFICIAL GOVERNMENT USE ONLY	
1. PW tracking number	2. Date PW request received
3. SOC (ONET/OES) code	3a. SOC (ONET/OES) occupation title
4. Prevailing wage $	4a. OES Wage level ☐ I ☐ II ☐ III ☐ IV ☐ N/A
5. Per: (Choose only one) ☐ Hour ☐ Week ☐ Bi-Weekly ☐ Month ☐ Year ☐ Piece Rate	
5a. If Piece Rate is indicated in question 5, specify the wage offer requirements :*	
6. Prevailing wage source (Choose only one) ❑ OES (All Industries) ❑ OES (ACWIA – Higher Education) ❑ CBA ❑ DBA ❑ SCA ❑ Other/Alternate Survey	
6a. If "Other/Alternate Survey" in question 6, specify	
7. Additional Notes Regarding Wage Determination	
8. Determination date	9. Expiration date

G. OMB Paperwork Reduction Act *(1205-0508)*

Persons are not required to respond to this collection of information unless it displays a currently valid OMB control number. Respondent's reply to these reporting requirements is mandatory to obtain the benefits of temporary employment certification (Immigration and Nationality Act, Section 101). Public reporting burden for this collection of information is estimated to average 55 minutes per response, including the time for reviewing instructions, searching existing data sources, gathering and maintaining the data needed, and completing and reviewing the collection of information. Send comments regarding this burden estimate to the Office of Foreign Labor Certification * U.S. Department of Labor * Box 12 - 200 * 200 Constitution Ave., NW, * Washington, DC * 20210. **Do NOT send the completed application to this address.**

Form ETA-9141 **FOR DEPARTMENT OF LABOR USE ONLY** Page 4 of 5

Case Number: [redacted] Case Status: IN PROCESS Validity Period: N/A to N/A

OMB Approval: 1205-0508
Expiration Date: 05/31/2019

Application for Prevailing Wage Determination
Form ETA-9141
U.S. Department of Labor

ADDENDUM

SECTION E.a.6a: Travel Requirements

2-5 trips every 90 days to one or more of the following countries: Israel, Thailand, United Kingdom, Germany, Japan, South Africa, South Korea and the Philippines.

Case Number: [redacted] Case Status: IN PROCESS Validity Period: N/A to N/A

ABOUT THE AUTHOR

Brian D. Lerner is an Immigration Lawyer and runs a National Immigration Law Firm for nearly 30 years. He is an attorney who is a certified specialist that might help in Immigration & Nationality Law as issued by the California State Bar, Board of Legal Specialization. Attorney Lerner is an expert in Immigration Law, Removal and Deportation, Citizenship, Waiver and Appeals.

He has been a licensed attorney since 1992 and started the Law Offices of Brian D. Lerner, APC. The immigration practice consists of Immigration and Nationality Law, and everything involved with and regarding immigration which includes citizenship, investment visas, family and employment visas, removal and deportation hearings, appeals, waivers, adjustment, consulate processing and all types of immigration and citizenship matters.

He has represented clients from all over the U.S. and in many countries around the world. One side of his practice is dedicated to keeping people in the U.S. and fighting for their immigration rights, while another side is to get people back who have been deported and removed from the U.S.

Also, there is the affirmative part of Immigration Law which Brian Lerner has helped numerous people come into the U.S. on business visas, investment visas, student visas, fiancée and marriage visas, religious visas and many more. Attorney Lerner has helped immigrants who are victims of crime and domestic violence or ones that are married to abusers.

In other words, Attorney Lerner has a firm that helps people all over the U.S. He has dedicated significant time to preparing numerous petitions and applications for you to get at a fraction of the price of hiring an attorney. He says it is the next best thing to a real attorney because they are real petitions prepared by an expert.

www.ingramcontent.com/pod-product-compliance
Lightning Source LLC
Chambersburg PA
CBHW082233240926
51846CB00014B/1436
9781958990032